THE VIDEO BIBLE

Revised Edition
by Barry Casson c.s.c.

Reviews

"Barry Casson has packed a lot of information about creating corporate videos into this 111 page book. A corporate video is an important business tool in this day of YouTube. The business owner could read this book and become the producer."

– The US Review of Books

"This book is a keeper, a tiny jewel. Every sales and marketing manager of every small to mid-sized company in the country should have a copy if they have even considered making a corporate video or local TV commercial…"

– DON ANGUS, Editor, Canadian Society of Cinematographers Magazine

"An excellent book for anyone who wants to understand how a film shoot really works. Peppered with illuminating first-hand examples from Casson's film and video making experiences. This book will save you a lot of time and money, and is a great read."

– TIM MOSHANSKY, Author, A to Z Guide to Film Terms

THE VIDEO BIBLE

Revised Edition
by Barry Casson c.s.c.

True Mint Blueprints
2018

Copyright © 2018 Barry Casson

All rights reserved. This book or any portion thereof may not be reproduced or used in any manner whatsoever without the express written permission of the publisher except for the use of brief quotations in a book review or scholarly journal.

Revised Printing: 2018
First Printing: 2007

Formatted & Inside Book Design by: True Mint Blueprints
www.truemintblueprints.com
Edited by: Carolyn Bateman
Program: Photoshop, Inkscape, Scribus.
Typeface: Bembo

Ordering Information:
To order further copies of this book contact Barry at the address below.

Barry Casson csc
#311 - 3277 Quadra Street
Victoria, BC, V8X 4W9
Email: bcasson@speakfilm.com
Phone: 1-250-721-2113
Website: www.barrycasson.com

Dedication

This book is dedicated to Alice and our great kids, Scott, Keith and Kareen of whom I am so proud. To mom and dad, Art and Eileen Casson my brother Kevin his wife Sharon and all their eight wonderful children.

Contents

Acknowledgements	7
Introduction	8
Chapter 1 My Circuitous Journey to the Film Industry	12
Chapter 2 Thinking Ahead: The Further Ahead The Better	16
Chapter 3 The Process: Five Steps That Make A Film	22
Chapter 4 Development: From Raw Ideas to Finished Script	25
Chapter 5 Pre-Production: You Can't Do Enough	31
Chapter 6 Production: What to Expect On Shoot Day	60
Chapter 7 Post-Production: Putting It All Together	82
Chapter 8 Distribution: Getting It Out There	88
Glossary Who Does What on the Crew	99

Acknowledgements

This book would not be possible but for the help and kindness of my friends. I would especially like to mention Carolyn Bateman, Andrea Spalding, Mike Rogers, Bruce Bachelor, Dawson Vandriel, Joanne Barker, Wes Barker and Digital Direct Printing.

Introduction

Film and video production have come a long way in the past thirty years. Film or celluloid, once the pinnacle of formats to shoot on, is now fading into the annals of history, though the word "film" is still being used to describe the moving image.

Today's digital technology now allows us to make impressive presentations through a variety of formats including tablets, or phones, instantly. You can do a presentation in your car, in the kitchen, in hallway. The phrase, "I'll book the boardroom" hardly applies anymore when time is short.

Having a film produced for your company is a tremendous opportunity to showcase what you make or do to the rest of the world. Nothing accomplishes this better than a polished, entertaining "mini motion picture," which we in the business call the corporate video. Even when your personal delivery is off, the corporate video never fails to deliver. Creative visual imagery combined with the right voice and emotionally stirring music is a hard act to follow for even the most talented of salespeople. And the best part is it never needs a day off, requires no expense account and can even do meetings at 2 am. without the double Scotch.

For over 35 years, I've been shooting films and videos for a host of clients. I've had my dramatic films aired nationally on television, and I have also taught film as well as shoot it. This teaching experience eventually led me, along with my partner, to open Casson Studios and Casson Film School some years ago. We then changed the name to Victoria Motion Picture School and added an acting program.

Introduction Cont.

We had the pleasure of teaching production techniques to students from all over North America and the World.

Through my production company Casson Pictures I've had the pleasure of being the camera operator and director of photography on a number of dramatic films with a few Hollywood stars. Prior to this I spent many years honing my craft as a TV News Cameraman.

As well as shooting dramas, however, I've shot, directed and produced more than fifty corporate videos. My clients include the Ramada Inns, Canada Employment and Immigration, National American Video, the Canadian National Railway, the CBC, CTV and countless other organizations. I've produced videos for small startup companies and large corporations, and I've received my share of awards from all the major film festivals in the US and Canada. I've also been nominated three times for Best Cinematography by the Canadian Society of Cinematographers.

Today what I love most is sharing this knowledge through hands-on workshops and speaking seminars about the film industry. I've provided these seminars throughout Western Canada to universities and high schools, film commissions, employment organizations and service groups.

Throughout the years I've been involved in the world of video production; two clear facts stand above all others. One: most of my clients don't know what I do. And two: they don't know how I do it. Through this book, I hope to provide you with some keen insights and some valuable answers.

Introduction Cont.

Today's corporate video is the mainstay of sales conventions, trade shows and the manufacturing industry, and it's my sincere hope that this knowledge will help you get a great promotional video that will increase profits for your business.

The way I see things, there are two very important points to keep in mind when having a corporate video produced. The first is exactly that: have it produced. Don't try to take a video produced in Alabama and expect your clients in New Brunswick to buy into the message just because it "kind of works." The second point is don't think your next-door neighbor with his little HD Handycam or iphone is going to save you a bundle by coming in and shooting video of your business on his days off. Trust me, it never happens!

In the following pages, I'm going to take you step-by-step through the process of getting your business a great corporate video. Many of the techniques I'll outline are used in the making of multi-million-dollar motion pictures. Though I'll refer often to the phrase "corporate video," this is meant to include all exhibition media.

Together we'll cover everything from that first germ of an idea to that first phone call to a producer. We'll delve into the script-writing process, including the translation of the written word into compelling visual images. In novels we think and feel but in digital video we must see and do. I'll walk you through the pre-production planning steps and, believe me; it's all about those planning steps. We'll strip away the glamour and facades that reflect the average person's view of film.

Introduction Cont.

You'll experience the hard work and dedication that goes into a great corporate production. You'll also get a look at the humorous side of the business and the crazy things that happen on shoots that make digital video production so much fun.

I'll also answer the most frequently asked questions in this business. Should your video be a half hour long or will ten minutes be enough? What tricks of the trade will allow the production to stay alive in years to come? How much should you pay for a good video? What's the best way to ensure the production won't interfere with the running of your business? How can you take full advantage of trade shows and use the video to increase company sales? How can you assess the producer's qualifications and is he or she the right producer for your kind of video? Together we'll look at these topics and many more. By the end of this book, you'll have an entirely new awareness of how films and videos are produced. We're going to pull back the veil and peak into that magical world of smoke and mirrors. "SHAZAM." Let's get started.

Chapter 1

My Circuitous Journey to the Film Industry

Just like so many other people, I've served my time in unsatisfying jobs. In my early years, being a great rock 'n' roll drummer was all I really cared about. My folks bought me a set of drums for my sixteenth birthday. They tell me it was the only time I stuck with anything for more than two weeks. I am sure the neighbors would have preferred the two weeks.

At eighteen, I worked as a hardware sales clerk-definitely not me. At nineteen, I became a junior reporter for a local newspaper. Good job but after constantly bugging my boss for weekends off for drumming gigs, he knew my interest lay elsewhere. In my early twenties, I joined a brokerage firm but that wasn't me either.

Finally, at twenty-four, I headed for London, England, to set the world on fire along with six other musicians, including a phenomenal piano player named David Foster. After a year and a half of touring, which included playing drums behind Chuck Berry, Bo Diddley and the Drifters, I found the fire had dwindled to a feeling of warmth and I was back home with a cushy nightclub gig six nights a week. It was at this point that I got my first introduction to the world of film.

I've always found it wondrous how a seemingly small event of little perceived consequence at the time can change your entire focus in life. This is how it happened for me.

Along with the nightclub gig, I was teaching drums at a local music store. One day the repairman approached and asked if I would like to buy an 8mm film camera along with a projector and a screen. Without a thought, I handed over $150 and threw the stuff in the trunk of my car. To this point the only clue that I might have something to offer the world of film was the documentary scrapbook full of still photos I had arranged to be taken while we were on tour in England and Europe.

Before I knew it I was writing scripts, grabbing friends as actors and doing some crazy little comedies that I would later show at the Christmas party at the club. It was great fun, but I knew nothing about filmmaking-or photography for that matter.

From this initial introduction came studies with the School of Modern Photography in New Jersey; seven years as a newspaper photographer, with an estimated 6,000 published photos; and filmmaking studies at Columbia College Film School in Hollywood. I followed this up with nine years as a television news cameraman with BCTV's CHEK Television in Victoria, BC.

It was around this time, while working for CHEK, that I got serious about shooting and producing my own films and videos on the side. One of the educational films I produced has been distributed widely across Canada and the US. Called Lost in the Woods, it was made back in 1983 and is still used today as a teaching tool by outdoor groups.

I always wondered if I could teach film as well as shoot it, so during my stint at CHEK I also started a night school course at a local college.

This teaching experience eventually led me to leave CHEK and along with my partner open Casson Studios and Casson Film School, which later became the Victoria Motion Picture School. I've always enjoyed the camera and lighting end of the business and taught this area at the school. It's been quite a journey so far and it continues. I often think of that memorable quote I heard years ago "Success is a journey not a destination".

Chapter 2

Thinking Ahead: The Further Ahead The Better

One of the first steps when considering the idea of having a corporate video produced is to formulate a clear plan of what your objective is. Like anything else in business, a well-thought-out plan will help the producer you hire bring about your vision. Spend some time on your communications objective so you can clearly get your thoughts across to your producer when you meet. In my career I've had lots of calls from individuals representing a variety of business concerns-restaurants, machine shops, hotels, prisons, the government, computer companies, you name it. They all want a promotional video produced. The one thing most of them have in common is that they know little to nothing about how our industry works. I've often discussed with colleagues how much time we spend educating the client about what we do so we can get us both on the same page.

Spend some time on your communications objective and clearly get your thoughts across to your producer.

A very important consideration on creating any corporate video is the prospect of updating the show a few years down the road. After all, new products come up and other aspects of the business can change.

So it's a good idea to prepare for this at the outset. The story structure can be treated in a way that allows you this option. This of course saves you money on the update later.

If, for example, you have the story constructed in a modular format, this allows you to take out some outdated information and replace it within its module with more current information. You may also decide you'd like to have a thirty-second commercial running the same time you have your completed video in hand. Plan this ahead of time.

Suppose your operation is in some way connected to a charitable foundation and that foundation would like to have a PSA (public service announcement) edited from the original footage. Planning for this in advance can save you a lot of money.

It's a good idea to discuss these kinds of questions when you make your initial preparations. I've produced a number of shows where this wasn't a concern at the beginning of the project but was raised as an issue after the project was finished. Now I always bring this up to the client at the beginning of discussions.

Give your video a longer life by staying away from specific dates and time.

It's also a good idea to stay away from specific dates and times in the video. Presumably, you want the show to have a long life and keep putting your message out. Once you start getting specific with date and times, the audience knows how old the message is. If you want to refer to certain new ideas and concepts, keep them generic. You may, for example, mention a change in government legislation that affects your business but avoid mentioning the year. Also watch out for T-shirts that sport logos referring to something that dates the show.

If your video is going to have a national rather than regional focus, look out for locally distributed calendars in the background or license plates that give away your area. An audience sometimes turns off if they can't relate to the subject matter due to location. Someone in the prairies might have a hard time relating to the message in a video when they see scene after scene back dropped by mountains that have nothing to do with the message and doesn't reflect their point of view.

You must also clearly identify who your target audience is. You can't expect one video to speak to all audiences, but you can make it work for more than one group. The safety video Lost in the Woods, which I produced a few years back, had good information for the general public. It also worked for Boy Scout, Cub and Girl Guide groups as well as in the classroom. Sometimes you can cut two different versions of a video from the same footage. Perhaps you want to target a slightly different group or you simply want a longer and shorter version. Doing this initially costs you more due to the re-editing of the show, but it will certainly save you money in the long run.

In summing up, have a clear plan of what your communications objectives are and design your video accordingly. Know your audience and think about the longevity of your video. Remember to include room for replacement footage and have enough footage to create a PSA or TV spot later.

Getting A Good Producer

You want to make sure you're getting the best bang for your buck so call around to several production houses. Make sure you have your questions written out first and don't settle for vague answers. Ask to see a sample of the producer's work. If you're planning on a video to promote a new metal widget your company is now making, consider a company that has a previous history with this type of subject matter. My TV family drama "Making it Happen" got me a lot of calls from organizations that were interested in family issues.

Ask to see reference letters from previous clients the company has done videos for. Make sure these letters aren't more than five years old. In our business, companies come and go quickly. Watch out for startup companies that claim they have done more work in the field than they actually have. This is a very easy business in which to conjure up a lot of hype. A few years back a company in my area appeared out of nowhere claiming they were working on twenty-three projects. No one in my business had ever heard of them, and we all wondered how they were involved in all these projects. I suspect they had written numerous letters to broadcasters, distributors and the like with ideas for productions. This is a very thin way to announce your involvement in the business.

Needless to say, a few months after their appearance, most of the equipment they had bought was being sold off at attractive prices and they were gone from the scene.

Try to find a producer with a previous history working on videos similar to the one you want for your company.

Chapter 3
The Process: Five Steps That Make A Film

As with major motion pictures, the process of producing a corporate video follows certain steps, though these steps will be abbreviated for a corporate video. The steps are: development, pre-production, production, post-production and distribution. Let's touch on them here so you understand the difference between the terms. Then we'll look at each one in greater depth in succeeding chapters.

Development

The development stage involves bringing together all the concepts and ideas and combining them into a finished script. From this, we know that everything works on paper.

Pre-production

Pre-production is the working out of all the details that must fit within the established budget. When and where will the film be shot? What's the best order and way to shoot? How much film, or hard-drive space is needed? What will be the established ratio of footage shot to footage used in the production? These questions must be answered. This is also the time to arrange for casting sessions if there are to be actors, hire the crew, rent the camera and lighting equipment, arrange for transportation and meals, as well as build and dress the set. These and additional details need to be finalized before the first shot.

Production

The production phase is the actual shooting of the show within the allotted time frame. With good pre-production, this phase should come off smoothly, especially if contingency plans have been made to accommodate some script changes due to unforeseen circumstances.

Post-production

This is where the show is put together in a chronological order that generally follows the written script. Audio levels of on-camera dialogue recorded on location are evened out. Sound effects are added. Background music is added. Digital graphics are inserted along with titles plus cast and crew list. All these elements are mixed together into the final show.

Distribution

The whole question of which clients should receive a copy of the video and which trade shows you'll exhibit the show at should have already been addressed by the time the video is finished. In addition, your producer may be able to point out other areas where the production may be of interest, YouTube or the school system for example and of course your website.

Chapter Four

Development: From Raw Ideas to Finished Script

I don't believe there is just one way to work with a client and produce a video. However, there are similar approaches that most producers would agree we all do. In my own case, it would look like this: I get a phone call from someone who has been referred to me by a previous client. The prospective client talks to me on the phone and outlines what they want. Generally speaking, they have little knowledge of what I do and more often than not they have not considered how much they would like to spend on the production. My job is now to clear up the mystique about what producers do and give the client some confidence about how things work. I take down a few notes and suggest we meet over lunch or coffee and explore the client's needs. From this luncheon meeting, I can get most of the information I need and the reverse holds true for the client.

If things are a go, I then prepare an agreement for the client to sign outlining what each of us will do and at what stages as well as how payment to me should be structured. Once the agreement is signed, I meet with my writer and discuss the project regarding subject matter and length. Next comes another meeting with the three of us as we flesh out further information. The writer then goes off and puts together an outline of the video. The writer and I meet for further discussion and then with the client to go over the outline.

Once we all agree to what is down on paper, the writer produces a complete script, which I turn into a shooting script. We must all be in agreement at this point. The client must be comfortable with us and with the story. It is a good idea for clients to initial the script once they have approved it verbally. This way there is no chance of a misunderstanding about what is being done. If any changes do occur before shooting, as the producer I would ask the client to initial those changes. The whole process to this point has taken several weeks.

Approve and initial the final script copy to prevent misunderstanding later.

Let's look at this whole question of outlines and scripts and how we move from one phase of the process to the next.

Outlines & Scripts

I can't remember the last time I presented a script outline to a client and had them say they didn't like the concept. This is not because I hire the best writers in the world, although the ones I work with are truly gifted. It has more to do with the client not really knowing a good script outline from a bad one. (An outline is simply a short narrative of the script without any dialogue or scenes written in; it is more like a story.)

If you are having a twenty-minute video produced, you can expect an outline to be in the range of three to five pages. This outline is the first step in getting both producer and client comfortable with the scenario. The next phase is what we call a rough draft. This is mostly complete but still requires some changes. At this stage, we have narration or dialogue or both (depending on whether we are having some dramatization portions). The final stage is just that, a "final draft." This is the completed script. This is the show on paper, and if it works on paper, you're off to the right start. It is very important that you approve and initial this final copy; this prevents any problems later concerning what is in the script.

The creative treatment involved in a script can cover a wide area. There really are no rules regarding creativity. However, looking back over the shows I've been involved in, there is one aspect that most of the scripts have in common. It is the wrap-up. Having put out the message in the body of the video, we return to the important points and re-establish them at the end. The old sales adage "tell 'em," "tell 'em," and "tell 'em again" is worth remembering.

Establish the important points in your video and reiterate these points again at the end.

Writers and I often get into discussions surrounding the differences between the words on paper and the images a producer, director or director of photography has to translate these into. There is a phrase used in the film industry, which is "And then they took the Alamo." That's only six words. Pretty easy stuff for a writer.

But let's take a look at this phrase from the producer's point of view. Well, let's see now. I've got 4,000 actors all in period costumes. I have cannons, guns, bullets, and my director has to bring them together in this battle. The director must think clearly about breaking down the script and taking an honest and serious look at the prospects of pulling a scene off realistically. With that in mind, a major consideration at the script stage is how long the video will be. The length of your video is an important consideration for a variety of reasons, not the least of which is financial. I've had a number of clients approach me wanting to know the cost of an hour-long production for their company. I usually give them the price along with an oxygen mask to revive them.

You can pack a lot of information into a video that is less than ten minutes long.

However, I find it truly amazing that in our fast-paced society, some people still think someone is going to sit for an hour to watch anything less than a superb documentary, Gone with the Wind Two or a very funny video starring a known actor doing the on-camera presentation. In this world of YouTube videos, It isn't easy today to get anyone to sit and watch a video for half an hour or even 15 minutes. Provided you aren't trying to capture something as complex as the taking of the Alamo, you can pack a lot of information into a video that is less than ten minutes and reap great benefits. Any salesperson calling on a client has no difficulty with the statement: "Have you got a few minutes? I'd like to show you something." Try this with a forty-five-minute video.

In addition, a video under a half-hour can sometimes work nicely on community cable stations, especially if the subject matter relates to community issues. Hosts of magazine-type shows need to fill half-hour slots. Showing a short video and discussing the subject matter with the head of the company can fill a half-hour nicely. Remember though that the cable station wants to reflect community issues, not promote your company directly. Short videos are also cheaper to mass-produce and consequently are easier to give away to the right client. I might also mention that short videos generally seem to have a better chance of winning awards than longer videos. This is probably because judges see short pieces as refreshing when scheduled after some of the more boring longer programs.

Short videos are cheaper to mass-produce and consequently easier to give away to the right client.

Chapter Five

Pre-Production: You Can't Do Enough Of It

Once a script is finalized and we know that everything works on paper, the director takes the script and "breaks it down," which simply means going through it carefully and identifying how it will be shot. The locations and talent required, the props that need to be found (a prop by the way is anything an actor handles such as cups, glasses, a wallet, etc.) and similar concerns such as this are all part of this very important "pre-production" process. Most directors I know all work from a planned script. The creative, visionary director who wings it on shoot day without a script is not what you want.

Most directors I know all work from a planned script.

My concerns as a producer also include insurance, model release forms, property release forms and the other paperwork that goes along with production. While I concern myself with how the script is going to be shot, my production manager handles all of the logistical details between my company and the client.

Quite often, I find that the client, though wanting to be with us throughout the shooting, more often than not is busy with the business and let's the crew do its thing.

I think it is a good idea during shooting to arrange your work schedule so you or someone representing you can be on set. That way, when questions come up, the director doesn't have to go looking for the answer and this of course saves time. In addition, you'll learn a lot about how all this smoke and mirror stuff is done and pick up a whole new language as the crew talks back and forth:

"Is that light hot? No, but I'll get on it right away. Johnny, get rid of the baby and stick in an inkie with a half double. Bill, get me two half-apples, some Hamburg frost and help Shannon with that spider. Where the heck are those C 47's? Is this the stinger you wanted, Harry? Boom that dolly down another six inches, Marge. Yeah, that's it, we can flag off the flare from here and slide in the net at the same time". (For an explanation of these terms, turn to the back of the book.)

So this pre-production stage is when we try to work out, right down to the smallest detail, how things will go once shooting starts. You may find yourself dealing with the producer's right hand at this point, a person known as the A.D. or P.M. We are talking here about the assistant director (the boss of the crew and the loudest voice you will hear on a set) and the production manager. The PM's job is to see that the show gets produced on time and on budget. Depending on the size of the production, a corporate video may have one person performing both jobs.

If the director needs your input at any time regarding the shooting script, you'll note that his copy has a bunch of lines running vertically down the page. These lines are his way of marking out the different scenes in the show. It allows the director to do his "coverage" of the script.

You can never do enough pre-production planning.

When we say coverage, we mean how many shots are needed to make this scene cut together in editing. We say coverage, we mean how many shots are needed to make this scene cut together in editing.

Now is a good time to point out the difference between a shot and a scene. A scene is really a combination of shots within a given location. As an example, consider this: A man entering a log cabin is greeted by a woman, escorted to a seat next to a glowing fireplace and offered a drink of wine and some talk. With dialogue, this scene would take up, shall we say, one page of the script. The director may decide to shoot the whole entrance and the sit down at the fireplace with the accompanying conversation in a master or wide shot showing the whole room. When this is complete, after so many takes, the director then has the camera positioned over the man's shoulder looking toward the woman. In this tighter shot, the actors would repeat the entire dialogue again. (Over the shoulder or OS shot)

Then the director would have the camera tighten up to just a close-up on the woman with both actors doing the dialogue over again and then a tight shot on the man. This "coverage" of around five shots, (not takes) total is what is needed to seamlessly make the editing of this scene work. Coverage is one more reason why shooting films and videos take as long as it does.

Now you may be thinking why don't we just use two cameras and save time? In a few general exterior scenes this is sometimes done, but for more intimate scenes where lighting is critical, the single camera technique is still preferred.

Earlier I mentioned props and I recall an incident when I was studying in Los Angeles that illustrates how important planning can be. I was working with a crew doing a television commercial for a savings and credit union. My job was to look after the props. It was one of my first jobs on a crew, and I was pretty green. One shot involved a young boy who couldn't see over the counter-top toward the teller but had to raise his piggy bank up and ask the teller to open an account. Just before we started, the director asked me to drive to downtown Los Angeles by the old Spanish Mission where vendors sold these clay piggy banks and get him a couple more   I returned to the set an hour later just in time to watch the last of three clay piggy banks fall from the young boy's hands and shatter on the tiled floor. If the director had not anticipated this, the whole production crew would have been standing around for an hour waiting for that clay piggy bank. It would have been costly to the producer.

Getting Your Money's Worth

This brings up the whole touchy business of money-how much a video can cost and how you can save money by doing as much planning as possible. It's difficult to give an across-the-board estimate of how much a video will cost. A producer has to deal with the financial differences in their clients' pocketbooks. The federal government can afford to pay more money for a video than can the guy just starting up his company.

I've completed a number of short and longer videos in the past and they have ranged in price from $2,000 per finished minute for smaller firms to $7,500 per finished minute for larger outfits and government clients. Please don't get the idea from these figures that a 30 second TV commercial would be cheap to produce. The gap between a small town furniture store commercial and a National TV Spot is huge.

Fortunately, with today's attention span, your video will likely be short.

Regardless of what you pay, you want your promotional video to have a professional look to it. A fellow producer once told me the story of a public relations person from a small city asking my friend how much it cost to produce a half-hour promotional film. (In those days, it was all shot on film not video.) Now, anyone in our business knows that whether you shoot video or film, not every shot taken winds up in the final show. The ratio could be anywhere from five takes to twenty takes or more per scene and only one of those takes would be used in the final product. (A take is the rolling of the camera and sound from beginning to end of a particular action.) We refer to the above as the "shooting ratio."

At the time, my friend told him the price would be around $1,500 per finished minute. The PR fellow said thanks, and my friend never heard from him again until he bumped into him on the street two years later. My friend asked the PR fellow if he had ever got a producer to do the film he wanted. Yes, he replied. I did it myself. Terrific, said my friend. How much footage did you shoot? Ten thousand feet, came the answer. Great, says my friend, how much footage did you wind up using in the show? Ten thousand feet, came the answer.

I can only imagine watching this show and thinking that my neighbor's slides of last year's barbecue would probably be more interesting.

How much do you want to spend? Many things affect costs. For example: how many locations will there be? If your company is housed in one location, then the production costs can be kept down. It can take up to half a day just to tear down and set up at the next location.

That means the budget needs to be higher because of the transportation and downtime as the crew moves from one place to the next. It usually takes a couple of hours just to tear down and pack the equipment in one location and set up at the next.

I recall one shoot I shot at a school that involved showing the correct procedures for handling a person who was bleeding. The school's medical room was not much more than a closet and was too small to shoot in. We simply found another room with a sink in it, rigged what looked like a bed in the background, put up some posters dealing with medical emergency procedures and we had ourselves a nice medical room. We saved a couple of hours of shooting time by not having to move the crew and equipment to another location. Shooting days are long days. Your crew is often hired for a ten- to twelve-hour day, and the director needs to get as much production out of the day as possible.

Keeping the number of locations to only a few will save you time and money.

Location, Location, Location!

I can tell you from experience how very important it is to ensure that locations are secure. Several years ago, my production manager and I were scouting a location for a federal government video. We were given permission to use a section of forest on land owned by a university free of charge. After two hours in the bush and excited about what we had found for the location, we headed out of the forest toward the road. A maintenance truck from the university was passing by and stopped abruptly. The driver jumped out and asked what we were up to. We informed him about the production we would be shooting in two weeks in this forested area. He then informed us that this part of the forest belonged to the Department of National Defense and was an old military practice range that possibly still had live mortars in the ground. Urgently inquiring as to the nearest bathroom, we tiptoed toward the road and noticed the signs that we, in our eagerness, had missed on the way in.

Experienced producers can always suggest ways to get what you want by "cheating" the shot. This simply means that the audience buys into the illusion even though the shot didn't take as long or cost as much as it might have. The industry used to call this a PMP (poor man's process shot), "process" meaning effects created through optical work, now it's an FX shot through digital imagery.

Let me just take you through how Hollywood does some creative cheating to save their productions time and money. We'll use the familiar people-inside-a moving-car-at-night shot.

Let's say you're watching a car in wide shot travel down a city street at night. This would be shot from the side of the road with the camera on a tripod panning the car as it goes by us. Then in a closer shot, we have the camera mounted on the hood of the car and we see the six occupants inside and hear their dialogue. The wide shot of the car passing the camera on the street is, in fact, happening on the street. But the closer shot is actually done on a sound stage in a studio.

Remember, it is dark outside meaning we can fake a lot of information. Our point of view from the hood-mounted camera shots is looking at the people inside the car. Behind them, through the back window, we see headlights from the car following. These headlights are just two small studio lights on a frame being moved side to side behind the studio car by one of the crew. Because they move, we are convinced they must be headlights. Every so often we see a bright flash of light, which must be oncoming traffic. This is simply a crew member with a light in his hand washing the car with light every so often to give the appearance of oncoming headlights.

The car on stage shakes a bit; this is another crew member with a 4x4 piece of wood wedged under the back bumper moving the car slightly. Often these scenes have rain on the windows, which adds additional atmosphere and disguise. In the finished, edited version, as the car in the wide shot that is actually on location makes a turn into an alley; we cut to the car in the studio and watch as all six passengers lean in the opposite direction the car is turning. It is convincing, has saved time and money and the audience has bought into the illusion. I once saw this stage shot done in only twenty minutes, from bringing in the car, lighting it, to the finished shots. This wonderful business is full of smoke and mirrors.

If you don't have a number of producers to choose from in your area, then you will be bringing in someone from out of town. Naturally it will cost you more for your initial meetings due to travel, and the crew will have to be housed and fed during the production. It is good to remember here that we are talking about corporate video production not Hollywood epics. Therefore, the crew will be much smaller. My crew varies from eight to twelve people on most jobs.

Anything you can do to assist your producer to get quality stuff in the can in the shortest possible time saves you money. You notice I said "assist," and I mean just that. Let your producer know that you are ready to make yourself or someone from your staff available to answer questions and help in any way to smooth the process. This person should be the one with the power to say yes or no to the questions that arise. A producer cannot get things done if he or she is dealing with more than one person with control. I always bring this up with my clients and ask them to assign this person for all dealings between us from the outset.

Assist your producer or director, but let them do their job.

The Partnership Way

Another way to reduce your costs is to partner up with one or more of your suppliers. Let's say, for example, that in your business you use a piece of machinery that packages or labels some of your goods. The company you purchased or are leasing this equipment from may be interested in contributing funds to the video. The end product will feature their equipment in use and they could use clips from your video to highlight their machinery in practice. If your business uses their equipment to a large degree, then they will reap major benefits from the video. They will of course want to have some input into those parts of the script that deal with their equipment, but remember they are saving you money.

This same idea could be applied to more than one partner. I'm familiar with several videos where this concept has worked very well. One of the video clips I use in my seminars to demonstrate this point has to do with a video about lighting tips while shooting on location. In this production, a parcel delivery warehouse was used to demonstrate some problems surrounding mercury vapor lights and their effect on the video picture. Clearly in the background of several shots was the name of a large national delivery company written on the side of several vans. I have no doubt that there was some "in-kind" or financial contribution made to the video.

There are additional types of partnership deals. I am not the first producer to approach a town or municipality with the idea of doing a tourist-type video, marketing the finished product together and splitting the royalty sales. In this scenario, the production company might ask for accommodation and meals for cast and crew while the shooting is under way.

The producer would have to pay the crew himself or ask them to share in the risk of getting royalty checks from sales. The selling price would have to be agreed on, and both producer and municipality would need to agree on how the video would be promoted, this being the essential point behind the video's success or failure.

Partner up with one or two of your suppliers to reduce costs.

Product Placement

Another way to make a partnership work is to be on the lookout for films that could feature your products. Perhaps your company manufactures hiking gear. Why not take the time to call around to your local film commission, if there is one in your area, and find out about any upcoming productions by local producers, television stations or outside producers of bigger films. You might find there is a corporate video about to be produced on wildlife habits and your product would be a natural for product placement. For some free hiking gear for the performers, any producer could arrange a shot or two that would feature your logo or name on a jacket, pants or boots, etc.

I've done a number of outdoor productions and approached certain manufacturers about kicking in dollars toward the cost of the production in return; I've featured their names in the credits as well as their product in the film. Remember, if you have a good video, it can be around for many years and be seen by thousands of people.

A good video can be around for many years and be seen by thousands of people.

I once produced a half-hour drama featuring some young people. In one scene they were drinking Coke. I went to Coke once I'd finished shooting and showed them some sample scenes to peak their interest-with no luck. "No problem," I said, feeling rather puffed up with myself, "because I've shot the same scenes with Pepsi."

The Coke people said fine, so I went to Pepsi. They didn't bite either. I eventually wound up with the Coke scenes and no contributions from Coke. Sometimes things work out that way. In general, though, I have always had good luck getting production dollars through product exposure. There is always a film or video somewhere that your product can fit into. Years ago one of the James Bond movies featured Mr. Bond looking at his Rolex or his Cartier or some other watch with the brand name showing distinctly.

Then we see a terrific explosion and we cut back to a close-up of the watch and then to Bond's face who delivers a line like "That's good time." I often wonder what those three words cost.

I was giving a talk some years back to a film commission in northern British Columbia. On the drive up I couldn't help but notice how desolate everything looked. During a question period, some of the locals wanted to know how to attract film business to their area. Thinking of the drive up, I was a little stumped for an answer, so I asked them what they had to offer. I found out that in this small town were seven helicopter companies used largely in the logging business. Now all they had to do was research films that were currently in the development stage (that first stage in the five- stage process) and contact the producers of the films that needed helicopters. They could find this kind of information in Variety or Hollywood Reporter magazines.

There is always a film or video being produced somewhere that your product can fit into.

Hollywood Comparisons

A producer in conversation with the client on the first meeting: Client:

"I saw this show on TV last week and it was all about the business I'm in." "It was a great show. I really liked the look of it. Can we have my video look sort of the same way?" "Sure," replies the producer. "We'll just have to up the budget by a few million."

The movie on television cost millions so we're really comparing apples and oranges. Don't expect the producer to deliver you the same results unless you can spend the same money. There is a term we use in the industry known as "production values." This simply means that what's on the screen looks like there has been a lot of time and money spent on it. You can have this same term apply to your video but within the context of your budget. Suppose you own a restaurant and you want the busy look in your video. You will need lots of bodies in the background. Do you have the budget to pay for twenty extras or will you settle for six or seven? Are you prepared to pay a bit extra for a skilled art director on the crew who can come in and arrange your establishment so it reflects a more polished look in terms of colors and settings that give production values to your video?

Do you have the budget for twenty extras or will you settle for six or seven?

I recently completed a short video for a foundation that needed the film to raise money for their cause. This particular organization helps to fund special trips for kids with life-threatening diseases. We were shooting in a bus with the lead actor, a young boy who is telling the audience about the number of kids the foundation has helped. As the actor looks around at some of the seats on the bus, the audience sees photographs of children who have been helped by the organization. The seats on the bus were blue.

Through discussion with my art director we decided to attach a yellow balloon filled with helium to the back of each seat that had a picture on it.

This simple decision to have yellow balloons against the blue seats gave the whole production an added dimension of color and design. This video truly benefited from good art direction.

> *Your film can benefit greatly from good art direction.*

A host of other considerations can affect the cost of your video, from using actors to what kind of format to shoot on. In the next few paragraphs, I'll discuss these in some depth.

Actors Or Not?

Professional actors can give your video a professional look. This is assuming you have a good writer who has turned out a strong script for the video. Please don't assume that the "outgoing person" you know in the front office would be the perfect spokesperson for your video. Don't get me wrong here. There is often a place for employees in the video, but it is rarely in the principal roles.

Your producer hires an actor for his or her professional abilities, which include strongly convincing your audience of the quality of your product through their performance. That individual from the front office may be a great talker, but put them in front of a camera and a director that demands a good performance on each take and watch how quickly your assumption of their abilities changes.

Professional actors can give your production a Professional look.

You may even want to contact a well-known face to front your video, perhaps someone that the audience identifies with concerning your subject matter. Sometimes you can get a local broadcaster whose voice people recognize to do the voice-over. They often do this kind of work in addition to their regular jobs.

What is happening more and more these days is using the voice of well-known actors to do commercial voice-overs. If you were to follow this route, you would obviously have to pay a bit more for the talent, especially if they are on screen and not just doing the voice-over.

In one of my recent promotional videos, the owner of the establishment presented themselves very well.

This person spoke well, had a good voice and wanted to be the on-camera spokesperson for the video. I agreed against my better judgment. For the most part, this outgoing, strong-willed individual carried things off. However, not having the acting skills to memorize and deliver several takes of the same scene consistently meant that, as the director, I had to use a variety of techniques to pull the shoot together.

The other problem was getting this very busy person on set when needed. This, of course, cost more production time, which means more crew cost and less profit. The real challenge came in editing. Because we had to use cue cards on the shoot, certain shots weren't usable because the audience would be clearly aware that this person was reading cards during what was supposed to be an ad-lib performance. The end product did finish up quite well, and in this case I think the individual on camera was the right choice.

Sometimes you can get a local broadcaster whose voice people recognize to do a voice-over on your video.

Actors in corporate videos do not have to be in a union, nor does the crew. The producer putting the whole thing together for you will often hire cast and crew with what we call "flats."

This means paying everyone for the day rather than on an hourly basis. The producer has only so many days to get everything into the can. If he goes over, then that extra day could be the difference between a profit and non-profit.

The term "flats" means paying the crew and talent a fee for the day rather than on an hourly basis.

Unless your area has an abundance of film production, your producer may wind up auditioning theater actors for parts in the video. Theater is a wonderful training ground for actors. However, it's not uncommon for older actors, who have spent so much time projecting their voices to the back row, to not come across believably in film. This results in a stagy performance and simply does not work. Acting for film is very controlled but appears to be much more laid-back. There is a term we use in the industry known as "the suspension of disbelief." An actor needs to be able to create this in the audience.

Suspension of disbelief is what an actor needs to create in the audience.

If your video is going to have actors in it, the director needs to hold a "casting session" when a number of actors come in and read parts for the director. This can generally take a couple of days. "Sides" (which are portions of the script pertaining to different roles) are given to an actor before the casting session. Other times, actors may be asked to come in and do a "cold read." This is when the actor has little or no preparation time. How and why someone gets cast is really up to the director. I often just get a gut feeling about someone, which I take into account along with whether or not they read well for the part. If you are giving input toward casting and it comes down to two individuals for a part, one who performs well but hasn't got the look and one who has the right look but is weak on performance, always go with the better performer.

A "cold read" is when an actor has little or no preparation time to go over the script.

In smaller communities, actors are mostly working part-time at their craft while a regular paying job keeps bread on the table. Getting actors for a three-day shoot during the week can create scheduling problems. Often they need advance notice to get the time off work. Of course, you can always arrange to have the shoot in the evenings or on weekends. The problem here is you need to have your representative on site after hours, which costs your company more money unless they volunteer.

In a documentary-style production, having a narrator do the voice-over is cheaper than having the narrator on camera. Mind you, a good on-camera performer/narrator leading the audience through the video can be a very effective way to get the message out. I've used this method quite a bit and achieved a good measure of success. Picking the right voice for the voice-over can also make a difference to the audience. Should your video have a male or female voice? Should the voice be confident-sounding or more friendly and inviting? It all depends on the subject matter and who will be viewing it.

An on-camera narrator/performer can be an effective way to get your message out.

The producer and director often go over some demo reels from different individuals who do voice-over work. I usually work with the client on this, emphasizing the benefits of each voice. Presenting the video to potential buyers of your product, such as other businesses, is quite different from having a general audience view it. If your market is local or regional, this could be an advantage, getting the audience to buy into the message due to the recognition factor.

Watch out for children doing voice-overs. Kids can sound great but sometimes don't speak clearly enough for some audiences.

It can take a director a bit of extra time trying to get the young person to slow down and enunciate the words in the voice-over.

Children doing voice-overs need to speak very clearly.

Film vs Digital

For years video camera manufacturers and producers have been trying to get video to look like the quality you get using film. The process started years ago with television video cameras using 2" or a "quad" tape format. This want to "1", then to ¾ inch (camera and recorder connected by a cord) then to Betacam, which had tubes like a TV set, then to Betacam SP with no tubes and then to Digital Video recorded to a hard drive and no tape. The quality we have finally reached has meant the demise to some extent of 35 millimeter and 16 millimeter film formats, though there are some Hollywood Directors that still prefer the look of film over digital.

I recall one of my students asking to explain the difference between film and video. I told him about how to see the difference. Film records the world in a wave type of format. If you draw a line on a piece of paper from one side to the other, but in the form of a wave with highs and lows, then you have the film look, gently distinguishing the elements in the shot in a rather subtle manner. Now if you record on video. Take your pencil and draw from one side to the other but do it in the form of a ladder with a series of vertical and horizontal lines one after the other. In my mind (and I'm sure most Directors of Photography would agree) film images are still much more beautiful to look at than those of a digital camera.

Compared to the cost of Panavision and Arriflex 35 millimeter film cameras of the past, today's HD video cameras cost much less. It all depends on the bells and whistles that come with the camera. Granted, for major television series and feature films, the extra technological bits and pieces are needed but not so much for corporate videos.

With today's digital SLR cameras and a host of other high definition cameras, you can create a high quality production without blowing your budget. Sony, Canon, Panasonic, Olympus are some of the big names in digital cameras.

Read up and learn a few details about today's digital video cameras and the kind of quality you want for your video.

Broadcast Quality

You may hear this term mentioned by a producer. It simply has to do with the technical image quality measuring up to the broadcast standards set by federals regulatory organizations.. Most digital video cameras today can offer high definition images. In our fast paced world though, you often see images on YouTube that technically don't meet broadcast specifications, but then you are watching these images on a reality TV show or YouTube or on some other broadcast medium where the content can outweigh the quality.

Images that were once unacceptable for broadcast are now being used in reality TV shows and other media programs where content outweighs image quality.

Images that were once unacceptable for broadcast are now being used in reality TV shows and other media programs where content outweighs image quality.

Insurance and Liability

Most corporate video production does not involve Hollywood stunts or cars blowing up and going over cliff faces. Nevertheless, film sets are busy places. A lot of equipment is used in corporate video production, and I'll be telling you more about that in the next chapter.

Everything from small to large lighting instruments along with cables, camera dollies, gripping equipment and the like can create a cluttered working environment. Some of the lighting instruments require more power than the average 15-amp circuit, and the gaffer or electrician on the crew will want to know if they can tap into your company power box to run lights. A reputable production house will constantly be concerned with safety on the set, but mistakes can happen and unforeseen circumstances can arise. It's important that whatever production company you hire to produce your video has the proper liability insurance. Most reputable production houses will carry insurance to protect cast and crew as well as third-party liability. If in doubt, ask to see a copy of the insurance form.

If child performers are involved, there are laws around how long they can work on a set and rules the producer is expected to follow. It's a good idea to assign a guardian to be with any child actor during the shooting day. Be prepared for long days while the shoot is on. A twelve-hour shooting day is normal in our industry, which means after four or five o'clock you will need a company representative or custodian to be on hand to troubleshoot and solve problems that the producer may have with regard to the location. You need to know that your insurance covers your staff and premises while unusual events like film-making are happening.

How Long Does it take to Produce a Video

How long is a piece of string and if so why? Once again, it depends on a number of factors. I've been approached by clients who discuss the idea of a video over a luncheon meeting and don't start filming until more than a year later.

Delays caused by people in head office having to approve things are not uncommon. Often production is delayed because the budget hasn't really been thought about until after our initial meeting. Now the money has to be raised.

If you don't need head-office approval, the timeline can be anywhere from one month to several months:, starting from the first meeting and ending with delivery of the final product. As with many business situations, the video's deadline can sometimes be dictated by an event where the client would like to show the product. As a producer, I can tell you the video doesn't always get delivered on time, but the additional time spent on production usually results in a better product. I used to make this point over and over with my students at the Victoria Motion Picture School.

I would draw the letter " P" three times on the blackboard and tell them this is what they have paid most of their money at film school for. I leave them hanging on this for a week or two until they finally beg for the answer. Then I go to the board and spell out "Pre-production Planning." It makes a strong impression on the students, and I can tell you from experience, you can never do enough of this.

What is the Standard Payment Schedule?

This depends on how your producer normally does business. I break the payment schedule into three or four installments. You can expect to pay anywhere from 10 percent to 30 percent of the full price up front. This protects the producer before the filming starts. This you will recall is the development phase and involves bringing on the writer and working out the script in conjunction with you, the client.

> *You can expect to pay from 10 percent to 30 percent of the price of your video up front.*

When I sign an agreement with the client (I like to call it an agreement rather than a contract), I get one third up front. Your second payment could come at the completion of principal photography (shooting the show) or in some cases after you have viewed all the footage taken. Your third payment comes upon delivery of the final edited product.

Often, the producer will show the client what we call "a rough cut," which is simply an unfinished, edited version. Seeing this does provide you with some comfort about how everything is coming together based on what you and the producer have agreed is a good script.

Chapter Six

Production: What To Expect On Shoot Days

Shooting a corporate video certainly isn't as complex as making a Hollywood film, but it's still quite a process and it's important to be as familiar with that process as possible. I'm not going to lie to you. Shooting can sometimes disrupt your business, and it's best to be prepared for this.

I recall a recent shoot for a restaurant owner in our city. We were to produce a thirty-second TV spot for his establishment. He didn't want to have his business interrupted and asked if we could work around opening hours. It just couldn't happen from my perspective. We needed talent (actors) that we could control, and if we were shooting during opening hours this would not be the case. "Could you just hold that piece of steak up to the side of your mouth while we put a light on the other side of your face and tilt your head up a bit? No not that far, oops, sorry about that." I think you get the point.

We wound up shooting each commercial between 9 P.M. and 9 A.M. with a day in between to sleep. We had to shill the restaurant with some local actors and individuals who had to sit around for hours and look like they were having a heck of a time. The owner had some concerns as well. One fellow who wound up close to the camera didn't quite fit the owner's idea of the clientele he wanted to show in his restaurant. Granted, this guy was two bus rides and a plane trip away from classy looking so we used one of the staff members to get the look he wanted. The great thing about this shoot, at the time, was shooting them on film instead of tape.

It cost more, but the client recognized the value, which doesn't often happen with today's budgets. In the end, the product looked great and I had a happy client.

On another shoot for a computer company, we rolled up with all our gear and started packing things in. You know the usual lights, camera, cables, etc. The looks coming back at us from the staff at their desks were as if an unannounced building renovation team had just dropped in on them. For some reason, after being very clear to the client about how things would go on shoot day, I got the distinct feeling they were expecting something quite different. I guess they thought I was going to show up with a friend instead of eight crew members, hoist a little four-by-six-inch camera onto my shoulder, walk up to each staff member, stick a lens in their face and go zip-zip, thank you, next.

If it were that easy, anyone could just get their buddy next door to do the video, and it might even look better than the vacation slides at the barbeque he wants to show you again this year.

A number of concerns can come up on shoot days. If your business is in a downtown area and exterior shots are needed where there is a lot of traffic noise, the whole shoot will move slowly due to sound problems. In major motion pictures, these sound difficulties are cleaned up later by having the actors redo the lines in a studio and mixing this track with a separate track of traffic sounds. In a small budget video, this is not usually possible. I was once shooting in a gorgeous location quite close to an airport. It was a beautiful day, the kind of day in which anyone would love to go for a walk or, as it turned out, fly his or her small plane. Sound was a nightmare on this job.

On another job, we were working at a house that was the perfect location for our shoot. Across the street was an empty lot. Sure enough, on the very day we started shooting, the lot owner decided to start building his house. I always tell my students that when shooting at any house on location, the first thing you do is check the length of the grass on the neighbor's lawns. You just know that lawn mower is going to start whirring right in the middle of the day's best bit of footage, and, if you have actors, it will be right in the middle of the best dialogue.

But You Said You Would Be Finished At 4 P.M.?

Don't be alarmed if the shoot doesn't finish on time. We work in an industry like no other when it comes to schedules. There is always another problem to solve as we go through the shoot days.

During the course of shooting a TV spot for a fine dining restaurant, we had to set up an interview with the manager in front of a fireplace for that warm and friendly feel. This was another situation of having to shoot while business went on as usual. This meant waiters with trays full of food speedily moving back and forth through the shooting area in front of the fireplace.

Now, I had been very careful in lighting this scene so that no one tripped over our wires and we didn't blind anyone with the lights. So, here we are ready to shoot. The lighting looks good, the waiters have agreed to give us ten minutes to get the shot in the can and now we just need to light the fireplace!, light the fireplace!, light the fireplace!. You got it? This fireplace, which had burned so nicely at other times, would not light for us.

We had to wait for the fireplace technician, and after one and half hours he got the fireplace to light.

Let me give you some of the more common examples of problems that arise. The office secretary we were going to have on camera at nine a.m.. phones in sick. That beautiful shot of the company logo on the outside of the building, which we all oozed over on the morning of the location scout, doesn't look so good on this overcast day. That new piece of machinery you wanted us to feature in the video, which worked so well last week, seems to be stuck in one position. The crew will have to move their cars because they are blocking the loading area and a big shipment is arriving in an hour. The sound department is having a real problem with the ballast noises from the fluorescent lights. They were fine when we checked out the location last week. We all agree that the shots scheduled for the shipping department are not going to work out unless we have more bodies doing things. We'll put overalls on three of the crew members and put them in the scene. The employee on the phone in receiving can't stop breaking out into a laugh during her scene. "Houston, we have a problem!"

In an effort to deal with the unexpected, I create lists of shots called "nice to have" and "need to have." This list helps me out when things get behind schedule. The "need to have" are exactly that. I can make the video work well with these shots. The "nice to have" are some of the more creative but time-consuming shots. My assistant director and I work out the schedule in advance, and he or she let's me know as we go through the day if I am on schedule, ahead or behind. There are not many production days when we are ahead of schedule.

So, as you can see, shoot days can be unpredictable. There are additional considerations and I'd like to run through these to give you a more in-depth look at what's happening during production.

> *The average shoot day is twelve hours.*

Safety

Most professional crews have cords of various sizes for lighting, camera and sound running all over the place. Knowledgeable crew members usually tape these cords down with gaffer tape. This stuff looks a lot like duct tape but is stronger. This prevents people from tripping and is essential for set safety.

Other devices may be used to place lights where it may not be possible to put a light stand because it will show in the shot. One of these is called a scissors clamp. One small device clamps to your office's T-bar ceiling so a small light can be attached. They are quite safe and shouldn't damage the ceiling.

There are always lots of stands around the set to hold a variety of lighting tools. You should see a sandbag or two on the base of these stands. This is to prevent them from being knocked over and causing damage to individuals or surfaces.

Film lighting equipment can burn very hot. If the ceiling is only eight feet high, lights will often be placed quite close to it. To prevent any blackening of the ceiling, a gaffer (the head lighting person) will often put a piece of "black wrap" between the top of the light and the ceiling. This material looks like thick tin foil and prevents any heat damage.

The crew should always carry a first aid kit with them. I recommend that you have your company first aid kits in place in the various locations being used.

The gaffer generally checks out your power outlets before shoot day to establish where he can plug in the lights without blowing fuses. No producer wants to have someone's very important computer information suddenly disappear because the power went off. If there isn't enough power for the lighting, the production company may decide to bring in a portable generator to run the lights. On small shoots, these generators are usually parked outside the location and cords will run from it to the production site inside the building. The only real problem may come from the sound of the generator throughout the shoot. It is mostly just a constant low rumble.

If your video is being produced in front of your business and public traffic has to be controlled during the shooting, the producer will need permission. For this he needs certain crew members to have an authorized traffic control ticket. Crew members doing this wear safety vests and carry stop and go paddles.

The On-Set Monitor

You'll probably find that your director and director of photography have a monitor on set.

The image may not appear as clear as in the final edited version because some on-set monitors don't have high enough resolution to display the quality of the video signal being recorded. Don't get overly concerned with the images from the monitor. Directors often view the action on the monitor simply to evaluate the performance and the blocking of the shots. It is especially useful for close-ups to see the actor's eyes and expressions.

The director of photography in some cases also sizes up his lighting from the monitor. A good DOP (director of photography in Canada or DP in the US) can usually work without the monitor, trusting his eyes and experience to get the look. This makes him or her valuable because they can move through the shoot without stopping to evaluate everything on the monitor.

For years, I've tried to get my students to use their eyes and not this small box to judge their lighting. In student productions, once the monitor is introduced on the set, the whole crew slows down because everyone wants to see how it looks instead of getting on with their job. Professionals are usually beyond this.

Waveform and Vector-scope Monitors

In addition to the regular monitor, you may also see two other monitors (usually very small). One is the waveform monitor. This unit simply translates the video signal into graphs on the screen. From this the director or DOP can judge the signal in terms of how it will finally look. The other is the Vector-Scope. This instrument let's one set up the correct color information and maintain it throughout the shoot. Not all video production houses use these on set. Good quality video can be turned out without these units.

The Continuity Thing

As you watch the production unfold at your place of business, you may notice that the script is not being shot in the same order as it was written. It is important to point out that most of the time films and videos are not shot chronologically. We may start shooting the last scene of the film on the first day, then move to the middle scenes and finish at the beginning. This probably sounds ridiculous, but it has a lot of merit.

The shooting schedule is based on a number of factors such as time, dollars and cents, availability of actors, of crew, of locations, etc. The production manager tries to put things together in the most economical and workable way to get the job done in the time the budget allows for. However, this can create challenges.

After editing, two shots may wind up next to each other that were shot on different days. Someone has to be aware during shooting that they match exactly.

The crew member responsible for making sure that scene to scene mistakes don't show up is referred to as "continuity." In my experience, the person doing this job is generally female. I think most guys will admit that women possess a greater ability to focus on detail than men. This job is the most exacting and one of the toughest jobs on set.

Major mistakes happen in movies all the time, even in big budget movies and it is "continuity" that has to look out for these errors. A classic one is the Roman soldier with a wristwatch in the movie Ben Hur. Another occurs in A Christmas Carol, made in 1951 with Alastair Sims playing Scrooge.

Next time you see this on television, watch for the face in the bottom left-hand corner of the wall mirror as Scrooge looks out the window on Christmas morning. This was supposedly a grip on the crew whose head sneaks into the mirror by mistake.

Can you recall seeing a movie where someone's cigarette is a certain length in one shot and is much shorter in the next even though hardly any time has elapsed, or how about a guy's tie done up in one shot and two seconds later it isn't. These are perfect examples of "continuity" problems. Even the best people doing this incredibly difficult job miss things, and we, the audience, catch them later.

In a video I shot for an education ministry, we had a male and female teacher walk down a hall and into a lounge area. This scene was composed of two shots: the first as they turn from the hall through a doorway and into the lounge; the second coming into the lounge and sitting down.

When I got to the editing stage, I found that in the hall shot the female teacher had a red purse and in the lounge shot entrance she had no purse. To make these two shots work together, I wound up going back to the original school location luckily, the original teacher could return to the location, and I got a simple close-up of her hand putting down the red purse on a bureau as she entered the lounge.

Fortunately, the lounge entrance was a wide shot and we didn't really notice the bureau in the background. This insert shot made the scene work just fine. I've worked on other films where the original cast member could not make it back for these shots.

In this case, we simply get the costume back and substitute another person's hand, leg or whatever to bridge the problem.

My first introduction to an insert shot was while I was working as a third assistant director with the American Film Institute doing a shoot in San Pedro. A fight scene on the docks had one actor slashing at the other with a gaffing hook. After the master and medium shots were taken, I got to do the insert shots featuring just my hand as I repeatedly slashed the hook into several pilings. These were later used during editing of the fight scenes. Come to think of it, I don't remember signing a waiver for the use of my hand in that film... Hmmmm???

Makeup and Hair

In some low-budget videos, this isn't given a lot of consideration. You can sit someone in a chair, put a microphone on them, set up the camera and shoot. You'll get an image that might even look passable, but it won't have the look that says someone cared about the image. Good makeup can make the CEO look like a CEO rather than a pasty-faced individual who hasn't seen a lick of Sun in months. A good makeup job gets rid of some of those zits and pimples and evens out the flesh tones of people sitting next to each other. The last thing you want in your video is the audience analyzing those pimples instead of listening to the message. Sometimes the makeup artist brings along a digital camera to check how the makeup is looking between shots, especially after an actor has been sitting under hot lights for a while and has begun to perspire.

On many of my smaller shoots, the makeup and hair departments are run by the same person.

Hair is generally not as big a problem unless we're getting into period pieces and wigs, in which case an expert is needed big-time for the shoot. Of course, if you're shooting outside and it's a windy day, your producer may have some serious problems such as the on-camera person trying to discuss something serious and looking rather comical because a strand of hair has been standing up throughout the performance.

I have to tell you, I'm always fascinated by the magic that hair people possess. Just when I'm ready to shoot a scene I hear, "Oh, just a minute, just a minute." Then he or she runs into the shot and, with outstretched palms, moves their hands around the subject's head as a flow of energy apparently bursts from their fingertips to correct the problem. I usually miss this problem and have never actually seen this flow of energy, but it must be there even if those magic hands never seem to touch the subject's head. I know this because they get paid along with the rest of us.

Sound

Never underestimate the value of good sound in your video. From the technical side of things, sound is one of the three most important elements in the show, the other two being performance and photography. Getting good sound is an art form. Good sound recorders (mixers) are always worth paying for on any shoot. They have a variety of different types of microphones at their disposal, which can be used separately or together on the same job.
The tiny clip on types that you see in interviews or on the news are great for keeping out background noises and seem to work best on women's voices. These mics are called "lavalieres" and are sometimes connected by wire to the recorder or camera.

"Shotgun" or hyper-cardioid microphones are the long thin ones that you see on the end of a boom pole. They have very directional pickup patterns, are as narrow as a flashlight beam and are great when your sound person can't get close to the subject. You may have seen these with what look like wool or feather covers over them. These covers are referred to as "windsocks" and help keep out annoying bursts of sound caused by wind.

Radio mics look like a lavaliere but are connected not by wires but by a transmitter and receiver. These can work very well when the subject is moving around on a street or in a crowd. They work best when there's no major interference with the signal such as a tall building.

On one production I found myself sticking the camera out a third-story window as the narrator, wearing a radio mic walked the street delivering lines to my camera several hundred feet away. This was a particularly difficult job for the mixer. Loud buses were pulling up next to our subject, and the traffic noise was horrendous. Whenever I find myself doing this type of shot, I always get a kick out of the passersby, who haven't a clue the camera is up in the window. They must wonder what is wrong with this person who is walking and talking away to no one and gesturing with his hands. Some savvy individuals recognize what is going on and immediately look around for the camera and, if they find me, ruin the shot by waving or announcing the dreaded phrase "Hi Mom."

If the producer's crew is working inside your building in a lunchroom, they will want to turn off the fridge during the production. Nothing is worse than watching someone do an on-camera interview and suddenly hear the fridge motor start up in the middle of the shot.

If the crew is working in your office area, their biggest sound problem is telephones ringing during filming. This isn't too bad if the phone is part of the background ambiance of your business, but if you're in the same room when it goes off, it is bothersome. Your staff, along with the crew, needs to turn off all cell-phones. In addition, the producer should address the problem of beeping watches that can go off in the middle of a take. They should all be turned off while doing a take.

Camera Filters and the Look

There are countless filters and other ways to soften the video image. In the old days of black and white film-making, camera people came up with the idea of putting soft, mesh-type material over the lens. They found this diffused the image slightly and got rid of lines on the faces of female stars. Today, some camera people still use this system, coming up with their own brand of mesh. Sometimes it might be a nylon stocking, dark or light. Today, that same principle is used with glass filters with names like Double Fog, Promist, Low Contrast, Soft Contrast, Ultra Contrast, Corrals, Chocolate and Polarizing filters to name a few. With these filters camera people can soften the image, make candles glow, warm up the flesh tones of on-camera people with pale skin, take out unwanted reflections and a host of other effects. We still haven't come up with the "thin filter" for that ten pounds television is supposed to add to your appearance, however.

You and your producer should discuss the visual look of your video at the outset to determine what will work for your business. I find that most often I am warming the picture up and softening the video image overall to make the show more inviting to the audience.

However, this may not be right for a video in a steel factory where cool, hard images could add to the appeal.

Lighting Your Video

I've never seen any production that didn't benefit from being lit properly. Yes you can shoot without lights and still get an image; it's just not the same quality.

If you have any kind of a decent production crew, they will have a range of lights on the set. Lighting takes time, and the DOP has a big responsibility to make your video look good. I often find that the director, the assistant director and the production manager seem to think this part of the job should happen much more quickly than it does. If you have a T-bar ceiling in your office, you will most likely have some form of fluorescent lighting. The color these lights emit is a crucial factor when the DOP is balancing his lights. Some fluorescents are what we call cool white, some are warm white, and some even emit a full-color spectrum. Often the idea is to add light but not change the look of things. Other times you may be asked to turn all the overheads off and the crew will set up their own lights.

You will, of course, see many cables running through your offices, and some of your staff may feel the heat from these additional lights. Depending on your budget, you may find some large lights positioned outside the windows of your business to shine like sunlight or moonlight. This is done because real sunlight moves all day, which means some scenes that may be cut together in editing, will have different shadow patterns. The production company lights usually stay in place as long as needed.

If your production is being shot outside on a cloudless bright day, you will have a high contrast range. This is called the dynamic range and deals with the differences in the brightness between highlights and shadows in the video scene. "Film" has always had a distinct advantage over video when dealing with high contrast but today's video cameras can deal with that.

Be aware that some cheaper digital cameras may not have the same ability to separate highlights and shadows as the more expensive cameras. When highlights are too bright compared to the rest of the scene, you wind up with waxy, overexposed areas of the frame. A perfect example is someone standing in front of bright window. In a perfect world, you should see detail on the persons face as well as detail outside the window. Your DOP (director of photography) should know how to get around this problem and make the shot work using fill light on the person as well as gels on the windows. (See Glossary at the end of this book.)

Any crew member that wants to tap into your electrical box to run lights should be certified in this area.

CHAPTER 6: PRODUCTION: WHAT TO EXPECT ON SHOOT DAYS

The device that looks like a small cell phone with a ping-pong ball attached to it is the light meter used by the director of photography. It simply allows him or her to measure the amount of light for consistent exposure throughout the shooting schedule. If you're taking part in your video, don't feel intimidated when he sticks this in your face more than once as he lights you up for your interview. This is quite normal; remember he wants you to look good too.

The Moving Camera: Dolly Shots

The idea of moving the camera while taking a shot has been around for a long time. The value of the moving camera is that the image on the screen is constantly changing and creates interest in the viewer. Your production crew will probably be using what they refer to as a "dolly." This is simply a platform that holds the camera while it moves. Names like Doorway Dolly, Western Dolly, Crab Dolly, Skateboard Dolly and Studio Dolly are familiar terms to the production crew. Small budget corporate videos often use a skateboard dolly, a square platform with skateboard wheels attached beneath it. Each corner of the platform has two wheels angled toward each other and these fit nicely onto two lengths of PVC pipe. At one end of the dolly is a push bar operated by the dolly grip (the person assigned to push the dolly). This system is light and easy to set up on a reasonably level floor.

The moving camera adds life to the video, and audiences are accustomed to seeing this kind of camera work today.

Another way to move the camera is known as "Steady-Cam" or "Glyde-Cam." This harness-type rig is worn by the camera operator and allows complete movement in every shot.

It's a wonderful piece of film gear but is not cheap to rent. It usually comes with the camera operator because learning to use one of these harnesses takes a bit of training, which you don't pick up overnight. Today of course we also have controllable drones which can have small cameras attached to get that moving shot.

When I was about to film Lost in the Woods (that children's outdoor adventure film), I spent many sleepless nights trying to figure out how to get a particular shot, which I believed was crucial to the film. In the story, the young boy is lost and has just made a bed of branches and leaves the way he had learned in school. I wanted the camera to go from the face of this seven-year-old boy, up into the trees showing how alone and vulnerable to the elements he was.

My problem was I couldn't do it from a helicopter. The forest was too dense, and there were no roads so we couldn't get a crane or any heavy equipment into our location. Now here we were, three days into shooting and I still hadn't figured out how to get my shot. I spoke with a few of the crew members about my dilemma. They agreed to discuss the problem over a few beers that night because I needed the shot in the morning. Here was the solution. They built a three-storey scaffold out of metal pipe. Then they ran two long pieces of 2 x12 Wood, down from the thirty-foot top of the scaffold at a 45 degree angle. They made sure the 2 x12's were adequately supported. Then they anchored a couple of long lengths of three-inch PVC pipe to the 2 x12's, attached a platform for the camera with skateboard wheels underneath that fit neatly onto the pipe. This whole unit by the way is called a skateboard dolly. Then they attached a rope to the back of the platform, which ran over the top of the scaffold. Now here's the clincher.

They attached the rope to a chainsaw, which instead of having a chain had a drum and pulley system in its place. I am on the dolly with the camera pointing into the young boy's face as he sleeps. They fire up the chainsaw, "rrrrum, rrrrum, Rrrrum." The drum turns, the rope tightens, around the drum and my camera and I start moving up the dolly pipe attached to the 2 x12's into the trees as smooth as you please.

Seeing this shot happen and looking at the finished product is what making movies is all about. I found the right piece of lilting music for this, my money shot, and in the final version we see my camera pull away from this poor little Cherub by himself in his bed of leaves and branches alone in the forest. I had to wipe the tears from my eyes. The topping on the cake came just as the camera finished moving up into the trees. We see a blue fog start to drift into the scene. It's the smoke from the overworked chainsaw, an added unscheduled special effect.

Why so Many Takes of the Same Shot?

Clients often ask this question while observing the shoot. They see a number of takes of the same shot, all of which seem to look pretty much the same. What you need to understand is that the director is looking for that one particular take in which all the elements of shooting come together. On some takes, the performance may be perfect but the sound recorder had a problem with a microphone. Or if shooting is being done on film, the noise from the camera running may have been too loud on the audio track. Other times a dolly shot may have had some bumpy parts in it, and the camera operator wants to do another one to get it right. It could be that the actor's performance was a bit stiff in the last shot and the director wants another.

I often find myself doing eight to ten takes of a particular shot looking for the right one. Sometimes a director can take the audio from one shot and use sections of it over another take where the visuals are great. Without numerous takes, this wouldn't be possible.

In one particular drama I was shooting, I had several scenes between actors lasting around a minute. In one scene, a husband arguing with his wife had to get up from the kitchen table, go into the bedroom, come back into the kitchen with his suitcases and then leave via the front door, all while delivering lines. This actor was so spot-on with his performance that I was able to take his audio lines from one take and drop the whole works into another take and it matched up almost perfectly.

Stock Shots

Stock shots are shots that have already been taken and are registered with a stock shot house or may be part of another producer's library of images.

Let's say your video is dealing with a new piece of equipment your company has produced and is being used on a fleet of ferries. It would be quite costly for the producer to rent a chopper and go out to get a beauty shot of one of the ferries as it glides through a bay on a sunny day. But a simple call to a stock shot house or another producer and there's the shot. The fee for using this image is generally based on how many seconds of footage used.

I once produced a film for a fish restaurant and part of the allure was to show many of the city's tourist attractions. The shot we didn't have was of the great fishing in the area. I didn't have the budget to catch a salmon so we bought one (the shot that is).

The three seconds we used gave us the moment as two sports fishermen hauled a salmon into the boat. A good shot and economical as well.

The Music in Your Video

A producer can introduce music into the show in several ways. They may suggest you go with an original composer or with stock music. Original compositions cost more and take longer. Stock music is simply a variety of musical compositions in different styles that have been cleared outright for use by a producer. Either royalties don't have to be paid to anyone or they have been partially cleared and the producer pays a small fee for each piece he uses from the library. These music libraries as they are called feature a number of digital downloads and CD's with music of different lengths on them. You can get everything from country and western to classical jazz and everything in between. I find going with the library music works best when you don't have large budgets. I have a tremendous choice and can spend as much time as I like listening to the different cuts. Many of these libraries feature the same cut performed in slightly different orchestrations and lengths. They also have "stings," which are just a few seconds of crescendo bursts of music for scene transitions.

If you have a good rough cut with no music in it, the show will improve 50 percent once music is introduced. Music can play big-time on the emotions of the audience. Dramatic upbeat scores can make the heart race, while a simple delicate piano can bring tears.

In promotional video work, especially for fundraising, I have always said that to get them to reach for their wallets they must first feel it in their hearts. The editor on the show should have a good feel for music.

Here's a word to the wise, about using vocal music. I find hearing vocals behind a video distracting because it is hard not to listen to the lyrics and this takes us away from the story. I've seen this happen on a lot of student films. A friend of the producer's can play guitar and sing and is asked to create the soundtrack. Often the lyrics have no connection to the video and compete with the video's dialogue or narration for our attention.

Chapter Seven

Post-Production: Putting It All Together

This is the editing stage. The editor now goes through all the raw (original footage) and makes a detailed log of each shot. The log contains information on the length of the shot, the performance if actors were used, how the audio sounds, whether the camera work is smooth, and so on. At this point, the editor may do what we call an "offline" copy with a "timecode window burn." This simply means making a copy from the original footage onto a portable hard drive that includes numbers on the screen that match the camera original footage. These are the time code numbers and reflect every frame in the video. You could say that every frame has a birth date and numbers that correspond to this date. The editor can use this "off-line" copy to do all the figuring out needed.

This approach is much less costly. By using your home computer, portable hard drive, or or even a DVD player, with a timecode burn, your editor does not have to tie up the more expensive editing equipment needed for playing the camera original footage to make basic decisions. It also keeps the original digital material safe.

You, the client can look through all the footage on your home computer and make notes for the editor on any problem shots you really don't want in the video. Now the editor links together the shots according to the script, keeping in mind any changes that have happened along the way. When this is complete, you have a "rough cut." The show now needs to be "spotted" for music. This is simply looking for areas where music will enhance the images.

Colors in the video can also be corrected from scene to scene in the editing process. Sunlight can go from very warm in the early morning to a bluer color at midday. If two scenes filmed at different times are put next to each other in editing, viewers will notice the color difference unless some correction is done in post-production. There is a rather humorous expression that gets kicked around in our industry: "We'll fix it in post." If a producer says this to you, you might want to get the details. With today's technology, many things can be fixed at the post-production stage, but only if someone is prepared to pay for them. Getting everything right at the start is much cheaper than repairing it later.

If narration is part of the script, the narrator is brought in at this point to record the narration. The editor then lays in the narration over the visuals. The next step is to mix down the music, dialogue, narration and effects into one smooth soundtrack. This process is called "audio sweetening." Finally, the editor lays in the titles and credits.

I've found that frequently, after the first viewing, the client will see a spelling mistake or identify somebody that has been left off the credits. I always try to anticipate this.

The finished length of the video may not be exactly the length the script determined. The rule of thumb is one page of script for each minute of film. I can think of several shows in the past where the final length has been a bit shorter than what the script called for. Don't be too concerned if the show moves too slowly at eight minutes in length and the producer wants to tighten things up to seven minutes. This editing gives you a better show. The feel and pacing achieved in editing takes priority over meeting the precise written script length.

Once the shooting is complete, depending on how your agreement is worded, you may be looking at the "dailies" or "rushes." This simply means viewing what has been shot. I must warn you that not everything you see will be a hundred percent. Like all businesses, some work is better than other work.

I once heard about an unscrupulous producer who came up with a rather unique way of getting around the sloppy parts of what had been shot. When presenting the footage to the client, he had himself, his editor and the client in a dark room watching the footage. On his lap was a clipboard with some papers and a light attached. Just before the bad stuff hit the screen, the producer would turn on his clipboard light as if to make a few notes. The distracted client would look over toward the light and by the time he looked back at the screen, the screwed-up shots had gone by. I can't imagine professional producing shots so bad that he would have to resort to resolving things through these tactics.

Enter the video in festivals so you have the chance to use the phrase "our award-winning video."

Who Owns The Video?

If you pay for it, you own it. You have hired the producer to make the film for you. This means you have the right to either distribute the video to whomever you please or to sell the video. Often the product is given away free by your sales team to entice new clients to your business. Assuming the producer has done a great job on the film, he'll want the right to send the video to festivals with the hopes of winning an award. This could also help you the client by giving your sales force the opportunity to say, "Let's take a look at our award-winning video,"

By the same token, once the producer has handed over the video, his or her responsibility for it ceases. The producer may write you a letter upon completion of the show stating how he enjoyed working for you and looks forward to serving you again. This letter will probably make some reference to the fact that the job is over. The letter is the producer's way of clarifying exactly that: the job is over. I am not the only producer who has completed a job only to have the client call me with some major change they need to the video within weeks of its completion. You can appreciate that the producer cannot accommodate this request within the previous budget.

If you pay for it, you own it.

Foreign Language Versioning

Sometimes clients need the video in another language besides English. In Canada, for example, it's sometimes a good idea to have the show in French. This would apply especially to national companies with offices in Quebec. At other times, it may be a simple matter of adding foreign subtitles to the video.

If you do opt for a foreign language version, your producer should be informed of this at the outset. It works like this. The final audio tracks, which consist individually of dialogue, narration, music and effects, are "mixed down," meaning they're combined into one track and laid onto the video. To do a foreign language version, the editor needs to keep the music and effects tracks (M&E tracks) neatly mixed together on one track with the narrative and dialogue tracks separate from this. (Effects by the way are things like birds tweeting, wind noise, traffic noise and other sounds.) By doing this, he or she can later go back to the original elements (meaning the video and several audio tracks) and replace the English narration recording track with a French or other language recording and then combine this new language track with the pre-mixed M&E tracks for the foreign version.

Without thinking of this in advance, the editor would be stuck with the dialogue, narration, music and effects tracks combined. This would mean re-recording all of the effects and music along with dialogue and foreign narrative.

I recall one video I produced where the client traveled throughout Europe and Asia and wanted his video to be compatible with the languages of several different countries. We created a modular type of program, and at the end of each module repeated a screen message in five different languages. I personally don't think this was the best way to handle the situation, but it was the most economical.

Chapter Eight
Distribution: Getting It Out There

Congratulations! You have your finished corporate video in hand. Why not celebrate the completion with some hoopla? You can build some publicity around the premier showing of the video by inviting not just your office staff but business associates as well. You lay on a little wine and cheese,, perhaps contact some of the local media outlets and you have yourself an event. If you do plan to contact the media, have your event on a weekend. They have fewer journalists working and are often scrambling for stories.

People within your business will get a real charge out of the screening. It can be a much-talked about event before and after the showing. Don't be surprised to hear a lot of laughter and giggles by your staff at this showing. This certainly doesn't mean anything is wrong with the production. We all tend to react that way when we see ourselves and our businesses on the screen for the first time.

When your video is finished, you have an event to talk about, so call your local radio, newspaper and television station.

Try to plan your event for a weekend where the media have fewer reporters and sometimes are scrambling for stories.

At this point, your challenge is to get the video in front of all those people who need to see it. I recall a computer company that approached me some years back. They were spending a fortune sending out salespeople to different parts of the country with briefcases, easels and diagrams showing what their company did. The airfares and accommodation were bleeding the company dry. Now, with their completed video, they simply answer requests by mailing a small envelope or allowing the interested party to download a copy of their promotional film.

At the time of writing your costs for duplicating videos of a video less than 10 minutes long can be as low as a few dollars each if you are ordering 100 or so, even cheaper.

There are many ways to promote the video. Many communities have business magazines that come out weekly or bi-monthly. These magazines are always looking for copy. Many of them have grapevine-type items that readers check to see who is doing what. Your announcement on the video should be there. Call up the local radio station, the one that has the talk show, and try to get yourself on there. After all, you have something to talk about. Announce the information on your website.

And don't forget about that wine and cheese party for all your suppliers and clients. You have a great reason to get them all together. Now, let's take a look at some of the final details you should know about.

Master Copies: The Original

The master is the final show, often saved on a high-definition hard drive or other Digital Media System. From this master any format can be reproduced. As with any business, the more copies you order the cheaper the price. If you have clients from other countries who would like copies, perhaps on DVD, you must first find out what format their country uses so that the video will play in their DVD players... there are a variety of different formats. Here in North America we use the NTSC format. In Europe, it can be PAL (a couple of different versions of PAL are out there) or SECAM. It is usually not a problem to have dubs done in your format of choice, although expect to pay more for dubs in other than the NTSC format.

I've found it beneficial to make two final master copies of the show. I give one to the client and keep one for myself

A number of times a client has called me two years after we've finished the show and asked me for dubs. When I ask them to supply me with the master copy, they found that the person who had it in their office no longer works for them and they have no idea what happened to it. If you don't have the master and there isn't a backup copy, it might be time to get out that 20 year old bottle of Scotch.

As a producer, I often inform clients that I can do all the dubbing for them at competitive prices. Not all producers have the facilities or equipment to do dubbing.

You should also decide whether you'd like the video to have a label printed up at the same time as the dubs are made or just leave the disc's blank. You may decide to do your own labels, perhaps with your company logo on them. Some videos have both a spine label and a label on the front of the video. It's a good idea to put the length of the show on the label. If your video is short, this tells the viewer how much time they need to invest and encourages them to take a look. You can have either soft covers for the video or hard covers (the plastic container type). If you're shipping them away, I strongly suggest going with the hard covers to protect the video. Accordingly, covers come in a variety of colors. Getting the covers to match your company brochure color is a great idea. It can look pretty sharp as you hand out the package.

Your video performs the same way each time, sending forth your well-thought-out message.

Festivals and Awards

Your video can be entered in countless film and video festivals both nationally and internationally. Most but not all festivals have a registration fee. The fee could be as low as twenty-five dollars or as high as several hundred dollars depending on how big the festival is. Winning any kind of award at a major, recognized festival can enhance the value of your video. You now have the credibility factor working for you.

Some of the more recognizable festivals include the International Film and TV Festival of New York, the Houston Festival of the Americas, the Chicago Film and Video Festival and the Golden Sheaf Festival in Yorkton, Saskatchewan.

You may want to leave the selection of which festival or festivals to enter up to the producer, who will be more familiar with them. You may also decide to split the festival entry fees with the producer. I recently completed a video for a client, entered the show in a festival and won another award. I immediately called my client and arranged to copy the award certificate for him, which he put in a nice frame in the boardroom. I have no doubt that his salespeople took advantage of the award when showing the company video.

Be prepared for a bit of a wait to find out if your video has won an award. Many festivals' entry deadlines are three to four months before the judging takes place.

Non-theatrical Distribution

This term applies to distributors of generally shorter films on specific subjects, Safety, Health and Education for example. These distributors will market to public libraries, service groups and the school system among others.

Educational distributors may often highlight a video in their catalogue by placing a gold star next to the title. This could be because the film has won a major award at a well-known film festival or had a very positive write-up about its value. It is a way of stating that this title is worth the price.

A distributor may hear of a film that has won a major

award from say a group like The Science Teachers of America. The distributor could track down this film for distribution to organizations like the science teachers and other associated groups.

A well-known fast food chain once produced an in-house film dealing with hamburger diplomacy. The video was about the efforts to open new chains in Russia. It dealt with teaching farmers methods of growing potatoes, bringing in cattle, the meat, the buns and securing supply lines. A film distributor went after this film for marketing. Though the video was made for employees of the company, the distributor recognized the additional opportunities to sell this film to groups concerned with how to build a business.

It would be a smart idea to check with a non-theatrical distributor before producing your video. They may just be able to give you some good advice on how to get your product into additional markets.

Winning an award enhances the value of your video in making sales.

Your Video at Trade Shows

There are definite benefits to having your video playing at a trade show. Suppose you are under the weather and just don't have the sales punch your well-thought-out message. It's also a great way to lure clients to your booth and often is just the icebreaker needed for the person in the booth next door to come over and say hello. By the way, when you do these trade shows, try to get your booth near the coffee machine or restrooms because this is where most of the traffic flows.

At trade shows, try to locate your booth near the coffee machine or restroom. This is where the traffic flows.

A good video can draw clients to your booth. It is important, however, to make sure that the viewing area is controlled. Placing the monitor inside a black, non-reflective area (velvet, for example) helps focus viewer attention and overall makes the product you have paid for look its best. Make sure you have a good monitor with the color and sound adjusted for your booth presentation. One of the real benefits of a good corporate video is that when someone comes to your booth and asked questions about your product, you can direct them to the video, with its strong production values. The motion, the image and the music can be a much stronger influence on the client than you can on your best day.

A major problem most presenters have at trade shows is the general ambience, which is often too loud and overpowers any audio from your video. If you turn your monitor up too loud, the guy in the booth next door will complain. So it's best to have the monitor enclosed. The image on the monitor is really the important thing here. I was at a trade show recently and couldn't help but notice the number of videos featuring what we call in the industry "talking heads." These images are about as boring as you can get. Nobody is going to watch, let alone try to listen. Better to have two minutes of arresting images then a half-hour of talking heads.

With a good video properly presented, you also have the advantage of speaking with one potential client while others are seeing and hearing the same message from your video. For the price of a dub, especially if you order a hundred or more, you can give someone really interested in your product a free copy. It is rare for someone not to take a look at a video within a day or so when they are given it free. A follow-up call is all that is needed now; the sales work has been done by the film.

In wrapping up, I hope that sharing my experiences in this wonderful business has provided you with some valuable insights into the world of film and video production and the opportunities and challenges faced by producers in the corporate video world. You now have a lot more information on how it all works and I sincerely hope your corporate video turns out to be the best investment you could make and brings your company a lot of business.

That's a wrap.

Barry's Film/Video Workshops and Seminars

Please note that I am available to provide a speaking presentation or one day workshops on video production to your group or business. I've previously delivered lots of these to chambers of commerce, colleges, media teachers and high schools in many major cities around BC, all with great success. See my website for more info and testimonials. www.barrycasson.com

Barry

My Topics Include:

- *How to Become Who You Were Meant to Be.*
- *How to Get in and Succeed in the Film Industry.*
- *How to Attract the Film Industry to your Community.*
- *How to Produce Your Own Corporate Video & Increase Company Sales.*
- *How to Shoot Video like a Pro (Professional Secrets).*

To contact Barry regarding booking him as a public speaker contact:

Barry Casson csc
#311 - 3277 Quadra Street
Victoria, BC, V8X 4W9
Email: bcasson@speakfilm.com
Phone: 1-250-721-2113
Website: www.barrycasson.com

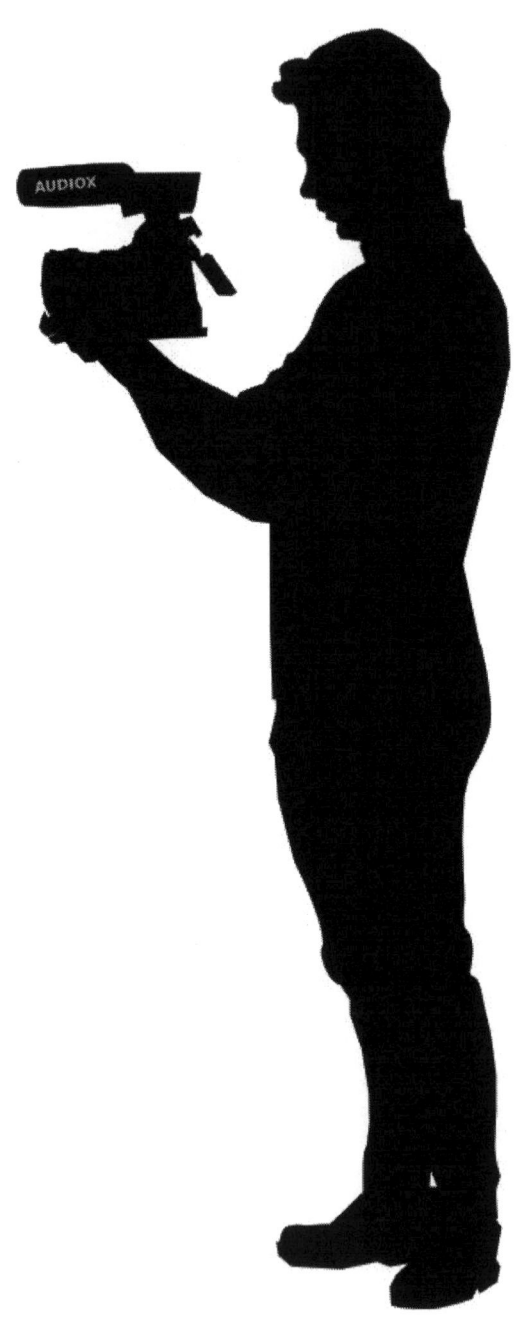

Glossary

Who Does What On A Film Crew

DIRECTOR
Responsible for the overall creative values of the production and is the head of the production team.

ASSISTANT DIRECTOR
The boss of the crew on the set and works closely with the director to help bring about his or her vision. This is the person calling for "quiet on the set" and "roll camera." By the way, it would be a good idea to alert any of your staff that may be in and around the filming to respect the AD's command of "quiet on set." People talking or giggling in the background can ruin a shot and cause themselves embarrassment.

PRODUCTION MANAGER
All departments go to this person for their budget allotment. He or she keeps an eye on scheduling, time and money.

DIRECTOR OF PHOTOGRAPHY (DOP)
Responsible for the overall look of the film or video regarding lighting and camera moves. Is the head of the photographic unit and on low-budget shoots may or may not operate the camera themselves.

CAMERA OPERATOR
Operates the camera, making sure that camera moves are smooth and that objects in the frame are meant to be there. Has to have a good eye for composition.

FIRST ASSISTANT CAMERA PERSON (1ST A.C. OR FOCUS PULLER)

Will take focus measurements and change camera focus. Changes lenses and filters on the camera. Makes sure the camera is clean both inside and outside.

SECOND ASSISTANT CAMERA PERSON (2ND A.C. OR CLAPPER/LOADER)

Changes film in film magazines or with video keeps track of shots on the hard-drive. Marks each shot with slate or clapper board (that's the plastic and wood object that makes a clapping sound in front of each shot to be taken).

GRIP

The crew member that helps bring the whole shoot together by setting up film-related equipment such as C stands, dollies, flags, nets silks used in the production.

DOLLY GRIP

Is assigned to the camera department and pushes the dolly (the moveable camera platform with wheels that sometimes runs along metal or plastic track laid on the floor.

KEY GRIP

The head cheese of the gripping department.

GAFFER

The chief lighting technician, who works under the direction of the DOP and physically puts the lights in place.

BEST BOY
The gaffer's assistant. There are a number of stories of how this name came about. The one I am familiar with involves a film being shot in England back in the thirties. A gaffer whose assistant didn't show up one day on a shoot got his son to come to the set and told the director "This is my best boy. He is going to work with me today." We also have best boy grips on a set.

SCRIPT SUPERVISOR
In charge of keeping track of the amount of film and rolls of sound tape used in the production. Also responsible for making sure that the actors say what is written in the script. If they don't voice the scripted lines, this is brought to the attention of the director who can make a decision on whether or not there is a problem.

CONTINUITY
The person charged with making sure scenes do not have gaping mistakes when cut together in editing. An example would be the actor whose shirt and tie are done up in one shot and unbuttoned and loosened in the next shot. We have all seen these mistakes in movies

SET DECORATOR (SET DEC)
In corporate videos, this is the person who comes in and tweaks the look of things on the set to give a more artistic appeal to the shot. They may rearrange pictures, move furniture or bring in items for the look.

SOUND RECORDIST (MIXER)
This is the sound recorder on set, and is often called a mixer because they are mixing the levels of different people speaking on camera.

BOOM OPERATOR
This is the person who holds the long pole (boom) with the microphone on the end.

HAIR/MAKEUP
Makeup can even out the flesh tones of actors with different complexions.
On small shoots, one person sometimes does both jobs.

TALENT
This is another name for the actors. When I hear this term, I am always inclined to think to myself, "What am I? Chopped liver?"

PROPS
Anything an actor handles (glasses, cup, etc.).

P.A. (PRODUCTION ASSISTANT)
This is a person who helps out on the production and could wind up doing almost anything from bringing coffee for the director to assisting one of the crew members.

Some Equipment Terms:

1K
Refers to a 1,000-watt light used on set. There are also 2k, 5k and 10k. lights.

BABY
Refers to a 1000 watt light with a Fresnel lens

INKIE
Refers to a small light of around 200 watts.

HMI
Looks similar to other studio lights but has a ballast system and puts out daylight color (very blue light)

4BY, 6BY, 12BY, 20 BY
Refers to large silks on a square frame (4x4 or 6x6, etc.), which are used over a set area to diffuse sunlight and lower harsh contrast.

SPIDER
This is a triangular piece of metal or plastic that attaches to the base of a tripod to keep it from slipping. (also called spreader)

A.K.S.
A camera department box that contains "All Kinds of Stuff."

C 47'S
This is the name given to wooden clothes pegs. (rumor has it that they were in box #C47 in an early times studios)

APPLE BOXES
Small wooden boxes used on a set to prop up furniture, camera or lighting equipment or just to sit on. They come in "pancakes," (very thin) quarter, half and full, all of different thicknesses.

C STANDS
Chrome stands used by grips to attach flags, nets, silks, etc.

DOLLY
A moveable camera platform with wheels attached. Sometimes runs on metal or plastic track that is laid down and leveled.

BOOM
This is the arm attachment on a dolly that moves the camera vertically up and down.

FLAG
A black, rectangular object on a metal frame, which, when placed in front of a light, blocks light from a certain area of the set. This is used to block flare.

CHARLIE BAR
A long and very narrow flag, that can be used to create a line of shadow when placed in front of a light.

BOUNCE BOARD
A large piece of foam-core or styrofoam used to reflect light into the subject.

SHINY-BOARD
A 4 x 4 board with highly reflected silver like material attached. Usually placed on a stand with a yoke and used to reflect sunlight It can throw light great distances.

FLARE
Light hitting the lens and causing the image to loose contrast

HAMBURG FROST
The name given to one particular type of diffusion material placed over a light to soften its qualities.

GEL
Colored gelatin attached to a light that can give the effect of moonlight (blue) and sunlight (amber) at different times of the day.
Windows can often be gelled to cut down the amount of light coming in on a bright day.

MATTE BOX
The black hooded item attached to the front of the camera. Usually has a compartment for sliding filters in and out.

SCRIM
This is a circular wire mesh device that attaches in front of the light and cuts down the amount of light.

HALF DOUBLE
Same as above but has wire mesh only on half of the scrim to cut light in that area only.

NET
A netting type of material on a frame placed in front of a light to take down the amount of light by a fixed measurable degree.

SILK
A piece of artificial silk on a frame placed in front of a light to soft

SLATE
The small black and white board that has the scene number and take number on it. Used by the "clapper/loader" to announce the shot as she claps the sticks together. E.g.: "Scene 34, take 5 marker."

STINGERS
A film term used for extension cords.

Some Production Lingo:

ABBEY SINGER SHOT
Usually the second-to-last shot. Named after a director who always said "This is the last shot" and it never was.

CALL SHEET
An outline on paper telling cast and crew when and where to report for the next day's shooting.

COVERAGE
This is the number of shots besides the master that it takes for a scene to be cut together well in the editing stages.

ROUGH CUT
The edited show that still needs more fine tuning.

CRAFT SERVICE
These are the people who prepare food and feed the talent and crew on the set. They may also handle first aid.

"DEUCES UP"
An assistant director's expression for the second take of a scene.

"DO WE HAVE ENOUGH INSERTS?"
Usually close-up shots of an action such as a hand reaching into a drawer.

"GET SOME CUTAWAYS"
Alternate shots not connected to the main action, which can be used in editing as a bridge between shots.

"KILL THE BABY"
Turn off the 1k light.

MASTER SHOT
The principal wide shot of a particular scene from beginning to end.

MODEL RELEASE
A document (often one sheet) signed by a performer giving permission to use the performer's likeness and voice in the show.

"MOVING ON"
The assistant director's term for going to the next shot in a sequence of shots.

PROPERTY RELEASE
A document (often one sheet) signed by a property owner giving the producer permission to use the property in the shoot

SIIOT LIST
This is a list of the shots in the film showing how they will be taken and in what order.

SPEED
The sound recorder or mixers term to announce that sound is rolling.

"STRIKE THAT LIGHT"
Turn on the light.

WINDOW SHOT
Usually the last shot and so named because in early film-making days, the crew would then go to the pay window to get their remuneration for the day. (window we get paid) yuk yuk.

"THAT'S A WRAP"
An assistant director's term to inform the crew that the day's shooting is finished.

About The Author

As a young Canadian Barry wanted to become an accomplished drummer. He did that and went on to become the drummer behind legendary rocker Chuck Berry on his tours of England and France.

Barry followed this by providing the solid beat behind musician Bo Diddley and also the band The Drifters on tours of Britain. Barry's close friend, music producer David Foster, was also part of this touring band.

His next career, as an award-winning press photographer with an estimated 5,000-6,000 published photos, led Barry to study film in Hollywood and upon returning to Victoria, British Columbia he received numerous awards for his educational films, TV dramas, and promotional videos. Barry's children's outdoor safety film "Lost in the Woods" (already credited with saving the life of a child) has been widely distributed throughout North America and was voted most popular film at the Chicago International Film Festival.

In 1989, with his business partner Donna Clausen, he opened Vancouver Island's first film school. For more than 15 years Barry Casson had the pleasure of instructing hundreds of students in the art of Cinematography and Lighting. His corporate video productions through Casson Films were nominated three times by The Canadian Society of Cinematographers of which he is a full member.

Barry's varied professional background has provided him with the experience and expertise to conduct his numerous film and video workshops, presentations to business groups, and talks to high schools, colleges, and universities.

Barry Casson's presentation "How to use Video to Promote Your Business" is well-received by Chamber of Commerce groups everywhere.

Barry's book The Video Bible (How to Create Your Own Business Video) is recommended reading by the US Book Review along with the Canadian Society of Cinematographers.

Barry Casson's signature Talk entitled "How to Become Who You Were Meant to Be" is the perfect choice for your next event, conference, meeting or seminar.

Photo Credit Steve Noble

Made in the USA
San Bernardino, CA
12 January 2019